Kindness in Winter

Kindness in Winter

Poems by

Sally Nacker

Cover design by Shay Culligan
Cover photograph by Gregory Hayes
(unsplash.com/@gregoryallen)

ISBN: 978-1-954353-37-4

Kelsay Books
502 South 1040 East, A-119
American Fork, Utah, 84003

For my mother

1933–2012

and my husband

Acknowledgments

An Amaranthine Summer: "Saying Goodbye," "My New
  Gladness"

Blue Unicorn: "Blue"

Hawk and Whippoorwill: "Kindness in Winter"

HOOT: "Poet's Garden"

*Mezzo Cammin: An Online Journal of Formalist Poetry by
  Women:* "Dry Spell," "The Visit," "Two Does in Snow," "The
  Deer"

ONE ART: a journal of poetry (Write it!): "David's Art," "North
  and South"

The Orchards Poetry Journal: "Saying Goodbye," "Old Age,"
  "Wonder," "The Woolly Bear"

The Sunlight Press: "Wild Phlox," "Japanese Brush Painting"

Contents

I came to learn my own compass
by sound around me on the ground.
I knew, I knew, I knew the grass,

the green blades, the widening mass
of hymns, or prayers, on every mound.
A poem's in a blade of grass.

Poet's Garden

From your study window,
you study every flower
in your self-made meadow,
hour after hour: bright bee—
in your own bellflower.

Saying Goodbye

If my heart arrests, let it keep arresting.
I kept thinking of your willed words
as I walked one last time that spring
to your summerhouse. Birds

hopped and sang in the thickets on either side
of Veery Lane. The green
world trembled so bright I cried.
At the end of the long lane

the small, screened-in wood
house stood. Something fluttered inside it
like a large moth, or could
it be a bird, I thought

as I came closer. I saw then—
its nervous movement through the screen—
a little brown house wren.
I propped the door open between

the green world and the world inside,
stepped in, and drew
close to the frightened thing, tried
to guide it toward and through

the opening. I could tell
the wren's small heart was beating
wildly, could see its little eyes, so gentle.
Then off it flew into the trembling.

Early Spring

The man and his wife live simply,
turning the wood in their wood stove.
It burns like thought and poetry
in the making, throws love

on the cool spring morning. Behind
their little house a garden grows
spinach and greens, the kind
uplifting faces of new primrose.

Dry Spell

Their song would hurt me—
the little sparrows—so I do not keep
the feeder out my window filled.
The clear drum hangs empty.

Where is the poetry I found?
Sunlight burns bright on the white
pine, shifting in intensity.
There is silence on the ground.

My New Gladness

Like the round bird and the rounded nest
the bird makes with the bird's breast—
      my new gladness.

Like the oval eggs the bird lays
in her round home where the bird stays—
      my sudden gladness.

The lightness of the roundness,
the birdsong against the soundless.

Blue

for Aleksis Rannit

Thomas Usman's trees are immortal
because you heard the sound
in them. Because you heard

the sound as being blue
and wrote it in a poem. Because you studied
the error of a speck of white

cloud on an otherwise perfectly
blue sky one day, and all around
that drop of white

the vast blue—wide like the sea—
world became bluer. Even wind high
in your neighbor's trees

was blue. So large a day
that was for you, so blue
with loveliness.

North and South

When I ask whether you have moved
upstairs, you tell me
your study
is in your basement
still, and though that sounds
deep and dark, you say
it is most lovely with big windows
looking south
across a gravel path
that cuts through a weedy flowerbed.

It is down this path,
you say, that yesterday
a little fox came running
toward you, then stopped
at the window
and looked northward
into your wildness.

Kindness in Winter

for Scarlet, age nine

Young Scarlet stands in deepening snow—
where she knows the doe
knows she has stood
before—at the edge of the wood.
The doe turns her ears toward the soft, recognizable sound
in the snow on the ground.

She listens from far in the wood—
and from a place of long-ago. Good
Scarlet feeds the gentle doe
red apples in the twinkling snow.

Old Age

Despite all likely lonelinesses,
illnesses, and losses,
my wish is still
to one day be very old—to sit
beside the windowsill
like now, and know
the birds that come and go—
to quietly observe the snow
dissolve into a field of flowers.

The Librarian

The gentle boy sought poetry,
told her he loved the wind and rain.
She asked, *Is it still raining?*
She knew him to be a poet
then. She filled with gladness helping
him find Sandburg on the long shelf.
They walked up the library stairs
talking about the weather,
striding through air together.

House Clarity

She slips quietly out
to a rain-wet bench
on the front porch
while the inspector
takes her husband
through this house they loved—
continuing, she imagines,
to point out its faults—
and she wonders
why people let wood
rot on their home, let
rainwater leak for years
into moldering rooms

when suddenly a pileated
couple swoops wide-winged
over to a hollow
high in an old tree
to poke for insects, quite happily,
without any noise,
and with such elegant
black bills, and striking red
crests she could look up
to here each day.

Two Does in Snow

Snow blew sideways; the sound was shrill.
Through the white air down a wooded hill
on which a house stood, a window
looked on two does in snow.

The does had entered a cluster
of trees where they lay under
and out of wind's way.
As though in a nest they lay.

For hours, they lay still.
They observed the wind with a poet's will.
Or to the poet it seemed so,
in the house at his window.

Wonder

for Leslie Schultz

Inside your own birdhouse,
overlooking a snowy view
unusual for late April, you
whisper poems in pencil.

Bird footprints in new snow
are like repeated stencils,
you note with your swift pencil;
a tale of a baffling passage

in search of seed and worm.
You write of bird concern.
In your heart, you burn
a light so bright with song

the birds must be looking in
to see what bird you are.
Your arc of human form, there,
bowed, singing, must astound.

The Woolly Bear

You wrote you spotted a woolly bear
just outside your front door, and you thought
it a sure sign of spring in the air.

I like the image of a woolly bear,
of your blue eyes widening at the big
black paws on your front porch stair.

Perhaps you thought, being the wonderer you are,
an enormous poem had come for a visit.
A poem, just up from a long sleep, there

at your door; hungry, with a desperate streak.
Over your coffee, you might have thought—
could it, finally, be the bear that you seek?

Summer Afternoon

My cat looks out the window there
from his perch into the air
beyond the screen that keeps him in.

From my reading chair I stare
into the stifling, singing air
face to face with my screened-in cat.

My other cat lies on the floor.
He naps sprawled on the cool wood boards,
oblivious to singing air.

We are three hearts beating. And
beyond the screen, bird-hearts beat, and
all the hot green world trembles.

Edge Habitat in August Rain

Where the Starfield meadow
and the wood meet the backyard, in a bright
red jacket she sat in rain.

The rain came down, drenching
her, and she heard it gurgle
through the house roof gutters

and down the gutter drain. Bird after bright
bird sang and flew back and forth from
the crabapple tree to the feeder near her chair—

that whirr in air like that, of feathers,
she had not heard before—they
flew as though she were not there.

She sat quietly in her straw hat, getting wetter
and wetter and the rain would not let up
deluging her in soppy happiness.

Wild Phlox

Phlox line the south side of the country lane
to the Teale house. They appear mid-August
and minister, with a certain zeal, in their purpleness.
Out of such globes of color, the five-petaled
blossoms preach a goodness and a fragrant
prayer. They ignite the air, and astonish,
congregate to greet me as I drive up,
and I feel so keenly my brief and only life.

David's Art

That day, I painted the sea at the seaside
where we lived in a small house
with a big window looking seaward.

I loved the wind and rain that thrashed
against the windowpane. I loved
all weather, altogether. I even thought

I was the weather; and the sea, I thought, was me
as my watercolors splashed over the paper, coloring
the blank world with a heaving and a tossing

of my own heart. I was a child, and I loved
that day at the window by the sea, looking
out at myself looking in at me.

The Deer

Through a veil of fog,
I saw a deer
crossing the quiet road.
We were driving slow.

She moved as though
nothing could harm her, strode
softly as a whisper
or a prayer through the fog.

I felt a blessing in the fog,
a grace pure and clear,
as we paused on the quiet road.
The deer was passing slow.

And then the deer, as though
she were a dream, flowed
away like water into the near
wood through a veil of fog.

Song for the Black-and-White Warbler

A little poem—
ink-black on white—
sings seesawing couplets,
high and light.
A little joy, a little fright—
a little day, a little night—
petite lively heart
contained in art—
it flits quick.

All in a Morning

I love the cleansing
rinsing sound
from sky to ground.

The spring rain falls
a long way down
from cloud to town,

crying wholly as it falls.
Over trees and hills
it falls. It seems its crying

will not stop, the pounding
incessant now on rooftop
and windowpane. Now

a calming quiet as it slows,
and again the sparrows
lift and sing in the clearing.

Japanese Brush Painting

Looking at it from indoors,
the sticks from the window improve the tree.
That is what art does.
      —Robert Frost to Robert Francis, 1950

The window makes art
of his magnolia tree—
the man thinks quietly—at the start
of spring. Especially

now, the way morning light
shifts—in falling snow—
over new white
blossoms on each long bough.

Window to Window

for Edwin Way Teale (1899–1980)

I would go to bed before nightfall
to watch the dark fall slow
over your writing cabin from long ago.
I looked beyond my windowsill

across your pond and meadow
over the cut trail uphill.
I saw from my pillow,
as night began to fall,

a ghost of you—flopping
your rolled-up shirt
about your back, driving
off deer flies—walking up the dirt

path, and heard, as my eyes closed, your
pencil—on paper white as new snow—
whispering secrets of nature
out your cabin window, long ago.

The Visit

Rounding the corner of a back road
slow, I saw a gentle doe
very close to my window,
tucked in a swarm of orange lilies.

Her head came very near to my car,
as though she were going to cross the road.
Then, in a slow-motion instant, her soft eyes
brushed my own gaze from a place far

and ancient, and I knew the deer
as she curved her neck and body
fish-like, and returned to the swarm
of the tiger lilies, so open and warm.

Notes

In the summer of 2020, the Connecticut Audubon Society awarded me a week of solitude at Trail Wood, the Edwin Way Teale Memorial Sanctuary in Hampton. Four poems in this collection are reflections on my time there: "Saying Goodbye," "Edge Habitat in August Rain," "Wild Phlox," and "Window to Window."

In a little drawer in Edwin Way Teale's study I found the words "If my heart arrests, let it stay arrested," written to his wife, Nellie, as part of his last wishes. These words, slightly adjusted, found their way into the poem "Saying Goodbye."

On a trail kiosk near Edwin's writing cabin are his words: "In the heat, I came up the hill flopping my rolled-up shirt about my back like a horse's tail to drive off the deerflies." A variant of this found its way into the poem "Window to Window."

"Blue" was written in response to Aleksis Rannit's poem "Loveliness."

About the Author

Sally Nacker was a recipient of the Connecticut Audubon Society's Edwin Way Teale Writer-in-Residence at Trail Wood award in the summer of 2020. She received her MFA in Creative Writing from Fairfield University. Sally has two prior collections—*Vireo* (2015) and *Night Snow* (2017)—also published by Kelsay Books. Her poems continue to appear in journals. Sally lives in Connecticut with her husband and their two cats.

Made in the USA
Middletown, DE
20 May 2021

40132527R00024